GEO

ALLEN COUNTY PUBLIC LIBRARY

3 1833 04942 8011

9/05

D0536047

Fishing for Numbers

A Maine Number Book

Written by Cynthia Furlong Reynolds and Illustrated by Jeannie Brett

Allen County Public Library

Text Copyright © 2005 Cynthia Furlong Reynolds
Illustration Copyright © 2005 Jeannie Brett

All rights reserved. No part of this book may be reproduced in any manner
without the express written consent of the publisher, except in the case of brief
excerpts in critical reviews and articles. All inquiries should be addressed to:

Sleeping Bear Press

310 North Main Street, Suite 300
Chelsea, MI 48118
www.sleepingbearpress.com

THOMSON

GALE

© 2005 Thomson Gale, a part of the Thomson Corporation.

Thomson, Star Logo and Sleeping Bear Press are trademarks
and Gale is a registered trademark used herein under license.

Printed and bound in Canada.

10 9 8 7 6 5 4 3 2 1

Library of Congress Cataloging-in-Publication Data

Reynolds, Cynthia Furlong.
Fishing for numbers : a Maine number book / written by Cynthia Furlong
Reynolds ; illustrated by Jeannie Brett.
p. cm.
Summary: "Using numbers and counting, information about Maine including
sweetgrass baskets, clipper ships, puffins, and state symbols are introduced with
poetry and expository text"—Provided by publisher.
ISBN 1-58536-035-X
1. Number concept—Juvenile literature. 2. Counting—Juvenile literature.
3. Maine—Juvenile literature. I. Brett, Jeannie, ill. II. Title.
F19.3.R495 2005
974.1—dc22   2005006127

This book is dedicated to my
1 and only husband,
2 loving parents,
3 wonderful children,
4 stately sisters and their families,
and to the countless but very special children who fish for numbers!
With love,

CYNTHIA

For my husband, Greg.
Special thanks to the Gear family—
Josh, Jenny, Elliott, Grace and Emma.

JEANNIE

1 fly fisherman
casts his line downstream,
catching a tremendous salmon.
That was like a dream!

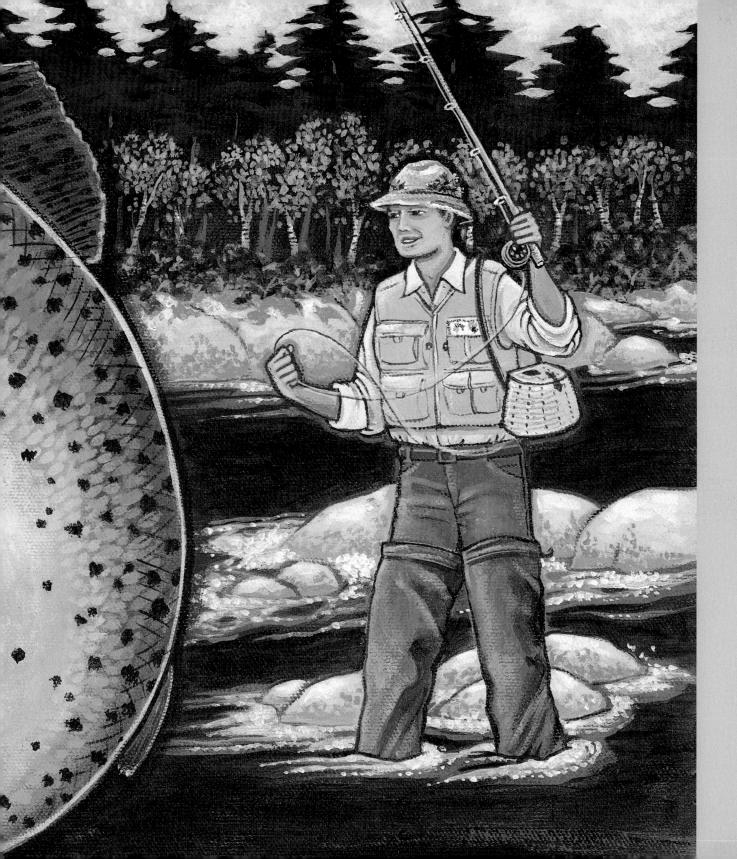

To people who love fishing in Maine's streams and lakes, there's no greater thrill than to reel in a salmon. As soon as ice melts from lakes, fishermen pull on waders, shoulder creels, and wade into chilly waters in search of Maine's State Fish, the landlocked salmon.

Landlocked salmon look like Atlantic salmon. The only difference is that one swims in saltwater until it lays its eggs. The other lives in freshwater and swims up mountain streams in the fall to spawn eggs over gravel pools. Landlocked salmon have black, x-shaped spots on their heads, bodies, and dorsal fins. Red spots cover the males' silvery sides. Their tails are forked and have no spots. Their backs are brown, green, or blue.

Long ago, Maine's waters teemed with landlocked salmon, but they nearly disappeared during the 20th century. Now salmon are grown in fish hatcheries and released into Maine's fresh waters. Landlocked salmon are hard to catch—which is what makes fishing for them so much fun.

one

1

Like lighthouses and lobsters, the loon has come to represent Maine. Once you've heard the birds' "Oo-AH-ho" wail drifting over the wilderness, you'll never forget it. Loons live in forested lakes and rivers most of the year, although they may move to the ocean during harsh winters when ice is very thick. Expert fishers and divers, loons have been spotted 200 feet below a lake's surface.

Loons are shaped like geese. Adults are black and white, 36 inches long, with sharp, pointed bills. They are built for swimming. Because their legs are attached far back on their bodies, they waddle when they walk. In summer, a white collar encircles the loon's neck and white spots cover his black back. In winter the colors change to gray and white to blend in with their surroundings. In the spring, loons lay two olive-brown spotted eggs in a cluster of reeds near water, usually on an island or a secluded point.

two

2

2 black-and-white loons,
famous for their haunting call,
dive deep in the lake for fish,
and dine just before nightfall.

3 sweetgrass baskets
 smell of summers past.
Algonquin weavers artfully
 make treasures that will last.

Maine's Algonquin-speaking natives, the Passamaquoddy, Penobscots, Micmacs, and Maliseets, are renowned for the sweetgrass baskets they have been weaving for centuries. They gather sweet-smelling grasses from marshes and the borders of streams and rivers, then weave the grasses into baskets. Traditionally, these baskets were used to carry everything: fish, vegetables, household goods, babies, and special treasures. The sweetgrass baskets hold their fragrance for many, many years. When you lift the lid and sniff, you can smell the fragrance of summers long ago.

The art of weaving these baskets and decorating them with beads or porcupine quills was nearly lost, but grandparents are now teaching the intricate and beautiful craft to younger generations.

three

3

4 fortified forts
protect harbors and ports.
They stare, unblinking, out to sea
keeping people safe and free.

The Maine coast is guarded by forts of all ages, built of wood, brick, or stone. Throughout our history, they have protected harbors and seaport cities from enemies during times of war—and Maine has suffered through many wars.

The earliest forts were strong log houses called garrison houses, whose second story jutted over the lower level. These protected Mainers during the 17th century and the French and Indian Wars. Later, more substantial forts were built to protect patriots during the American Revolution and the War of 1812. Fort Preble in the Casco Bay and Fort Knox at Bucksport were constructed when the Civil War began. Fort Williams in Cape Elizabeth is a 20th-century fort designed to protect Americans during the two World Wars. Nowadays, Maine has 20 forts remaining along the coast from Kittery to Machias and inland along the Kennebec and St. John's rivers.

four

4

The Atlantic puffin's scientific name, *fratercula artica*, means "little brother of the north." Puffins look like cuddly cartoon characters. They have white feather bibs over their rounded tummies; their backs are black; their thick curved beaks and webbed feet are bright orange.

Puffins are skillful swimmers, fishers, and fliers (up to 50 miles an hour). For nine months they live at sea then they cuddle in puffin colonies, making their homes in rock crevices or burrows. Puffin couples don't always live together, but they always meet in spring. They lay one pointed egg that hatches in 40 days. Both parents raise the baby. The baby learns to identify its home by a process called imprinting. When not quite grown, the pufflings fly away. After two years at sea they return home.

Puffins can live for 25 years. It's easy to tell their age by looking at the grooves on their orange beaks—one groove represents two years. Stephen Kress's Project Puffin began reintroducing the nearly extinct birds to Maine in 1973. Today at least four islands shelter puffin breeding colonies.

five
5

5 puckish puffins,
      black, white, and sleek,
   look like identical twins
            playing hide and seek.

3 1822 04942 8011

6 marvelous miniature Mayflowers
signal the coming of spring.
When flurries turn to showers,
they're a gift that sweethearts bring.

Mayflower is another name for Trailing Arbutus. The tiny clusters of pink and white spicy-smelling flowers appear early in spring, just as the last of the snows are melting in Maine. The Mayflower is an evergreen wildflower that can be found along the edges of Maine's woodlands, although the blooms are becoming scarcer and people are now asked not to pick them.

Long ago in Maine, children and sweethearts crafted May Day baskets out of rushes or paper. They filled them with Mayflowers, sweets, and a poem or riddle, then early on May Day morning (May 1), they would sneak the gifts onto doorsteps. After knocking, they ran and hid, peeking to see if the right person found the basket.

six

6

Sardines are little fish found all over the world, sometimes in tremendous schools, or clusters. Toothless, with long, thin little bodies and oily flesh, they are a very healthy food.

Once, sardine factories lined the coast of Maine to process and can the millions of sardines fishermen brought. In the early years of the 20th century, Maine fishermen caught as many as 13 million tons of sardines each year. Women and children worked in the factories, cutting off fish heads and packing the sardines into cans. Until 1972, sardines were the largest catch in Maine, but when their numbers began dropping, sardine factories began closing.

7 silly sardines
form a little school.
They never have to add or spell
in their shimmering, salty pool.

seven

7

Maine's shipbuilders have always ranked among the best in the world. The first recorded American ship was built in Maine in 1607. In the early 1800s, Maine's shipbuilders launched three-masted commercial ships that sailed so quickly they were said to "clip off" the knots, or miles. These were called clipper ships. Built for speed, the clipper ship was long and slim, with soaring masts and many tall sails. Because they were so fast, they were sent to China to bring back the season's tea and to Europe with important messages and documents. Clipper ships also competed with the wagon trains to bring Gold Rush passengers to California quickly. In time, however, windjammers replaced clipper ships because they could hold much more cargo.

You can learn about Maine's maritime history at the Maine Maritime Museum in Bath and the Penobscot Marine Museum in Searsport. Maine still has many fine boat builders and Maine's sailors are still famous for their skills.

eight

8

8 elegant clipper ships
glide serenely on the breeze.
No faster wooden ships ever sailed.
They raced pirates on the high seas.

9 cuddly coon cats
　　play a cat-and-mouse game.
　　History, size, and breeding
bring them attention and fame.

Known as the "Gentle Giant" of the cat world, the Maine coon cat is the only domestic cat native to North America. Most breeders believe that the coon cat resulted from matings between shorthaired native American cats and longhaired domesticated cats (perhaps Angora) brought to these shores either by English seamen or Vikings.

The Maine coon is well adapted to our harsh climate. No other breed has such a glossy, heavy, water-resistant coat. Its hair is longer on the ruff, stomach, and legs to protect against wet and snow; shorter hair on the back and neck help the cats avoid entangling underbrush. When they sleep, coons wrap their long, bushy tails around themselves as protection from the cold. Ears are heavily furred for warmth. Big, round, tufted feet serve as snow shoes. Their sight and hearing are excellent. Full-grown coon cats can weigh 18 pounds.

nine
9

In the days when Maine was part of Massachusetts and Massachusetts was a British colony, the king decreed that the tallest, straightest, strongest trees in the Maine woods belonged to him. More than 225 years ago, the king sent foresters into the woods to brand the best trees with a broad arrow mark; they were to be cut and used as masts for the kings' ships. Some of those very old trees were never cut down. They still stand deep in the wilderness as monuments to exciting days in Maine's past. Foresters hope that they will survive for a very, very long time.

ten

10

10 tall, thick pine trees,
marked with the king's broad arrows,
hide alone in the wilderness,
known only to squirrels and sparrows.

11 lumbering lumberjacks
took axes and saws to the wood.
Long ago, they spent the winter there,
cutting all the pines they could.

Because Maine is covered in forests, the lumber business has always been very important here. Nowadays, men use big machines to cut trees and load the logs onto long trucks, which carry them to sawmills and paper mills. But once upon a time, men called lumberjacks or loggers spent all winter living in camps deep in the woods, felling trees with axes and saws. The logs were loaded by hand or winches onto large flat sleighs. Oxen dragged the sleighs across rough frozen roads to the side of a lake or river where they were stored until spring. When the ice melted and rivers flowed their fastest, logs were floated to sawmills or ships on a "log drive."

Some lumberjacks became famous for their strength and speed with axes and with their skills in jumping from log to log as they bounced and rolled down rapid rivers. One of America's favorite folk heroes is Paul Bunyan, a giant lumberjack whose stories date to the mid-1800s. His statue stands larger than life in Bangor.

eleven
11

There are many kinds of buoys (pronounced BOO-EES) floating in Maine's waters. Some guide ships into harbors with lights. Others warn of dangerous rocks, sand bars, or shallows. Rocked by waves, bell buoys ring to alert sailors about dangers. Lobstermen have their own special kind of buoys, which are smaller, and brightly painted in special ways. Attached by ropes to lobster pots, they mark spots where fishermen place their traps in the ocean. When lobstermen see other buoys' colors, they know where their friends are fishing.

Early settlers reported seeing lobsters eight feet long. Historically they were considered food for poor people. Prisoners and servants often complained because they had to eat so much lobster, but by the 1920s lobster was regarded as a luxury food. The Burnham & Morrill Company of Portland, B&M, started canning lobster for sale around the world. Maine fishermen trap 90 percent of all lobsters eaten in the U.S.

twelve
12

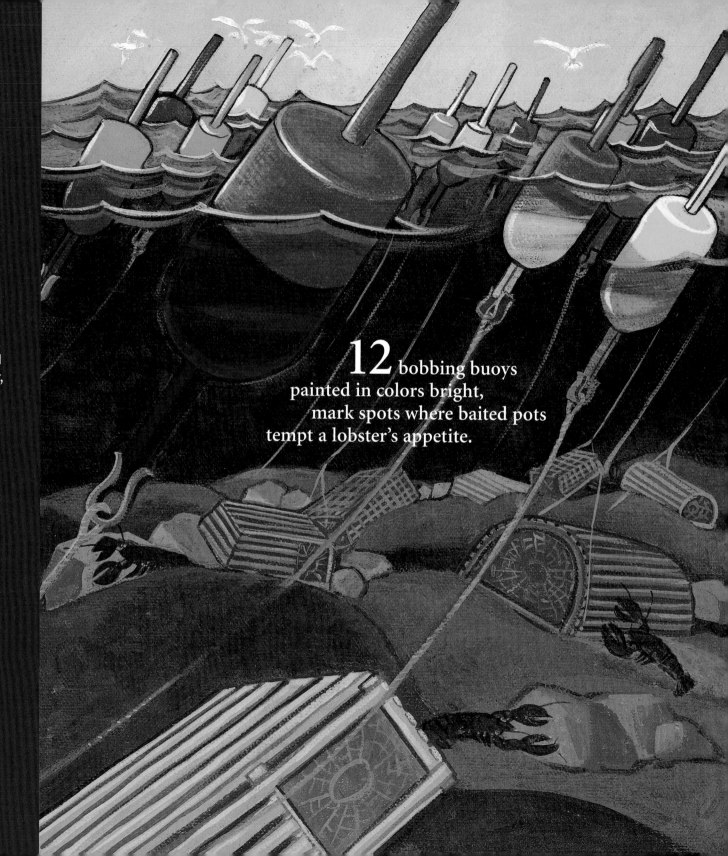

12 bobbing buoys
painted in colors bright,
mark spots where baited pots
tempt a lobster's appetite.

Usually a dozen is 12 of anything, but bakers add one extra to their dozen as a special treat. A baker's dozen is always 13. Maine boasts wonderful bakers, and pies are their specialties. Long ago, women spent one whole day every week baking pies and breads, which their families ate for breakfast, lunch and dinner. County fairs still hold baking contests, offering blue ribbons to the best bakers.

Blueberries have always grown wild in Maine. Today they are cultivated, to give people everywhere the fattest, sweetest, juiciest berries. Growers burn fields to prepare them, then bring in bee hives to pollinate the little blueberry flowers. Short-handled rakes help pickers collect the berries as fast as they can.

The blueberry barrens of Washington and Hancock counties cover 60,000 acres. When the berries are ripe, the fields look as blue as the ocean. Cherryfield is "The Blueberry Capital of the World." More than 98 percent of our nation's lowbush blueberries are harvested nearby.

thirteen
13

13 bustling bakers
pick berries as blue as the skies.
Then they mix, roll, and bake
dozens of blueberry pies.

In the 19th century when shipyards lined the Maine coast, the Friendship Sloop was created to fit the needs of Muscongus Bay fishermen. Between 30 and 40 feet long with an elliptical stern and a clipper bow, Friendship Sloops cut through the water masterfully. Fishermen used them when they dropped nets for herring and fished for sword fish, lobsters, cod, and mackerel.

Shipbuilders went into the forests to cut timbers, hauled the timbers to sawmills, then floated sawn planks to offshore boathouses. As the ships were being built, shipbuilders spread sailcloth in fields and cut sail pieces, which their wives sewed together. Some sloops were dragged onto the ice in spring and left there until the ice melted and they could float. Oxen hauled others to the water. Although many coastal families built these ships, Wilbur Morse is considered the father of the Friendship Sloop because he built so many. His shop was in Friendship.

fourteen
14

14 Friendship Sloops
built for fishermen long ago,
were launched into the ocean
with mighty shouts, "Heave ho!"

15 wily whales
glide serenely across the sea.
Flapping flippers and flat tails,
they dive and swim carefree.

From Kittery to Eastport, ships offer day trips to passengers who hope to glimpse Maine's largest mammals: humpback, finback, right, and minke whales. The minkes are the smallest whales in our waters, at 30 feet long; the finbacks are longest at 80 feet.

Scientists believe that whales are related to the hippopotamus. Like other mammals, whales are warm-blooded, breathe air, and produce milk to feed their babies. Whales have excellent vision and hearing. Females give birth to one calf every two or three years.

Whales' streamlined bodies have insulating layers of blubber. Flippers and a flat tail propel the whale through the water. A whale's head is huge—and so is its mouth. It takes a lot of small fish and plankton to fill this animal. Blowholes, located on the top of the whale's head, are nostril openings. Most whales must surface at least every twenty minutes to take a breath. Spouting water empties their blowholes so whales can breathe.

fifteen

15

Incredibly skillful swimmers, seals always seem to be having fun as they splash and glide along Maine's shores. Unlike tourists, seals prefer chilly seawater. They have streamlined bodies and webbed flippers, allowing them to move effortlessly in water, but awkwardly on land. A thick layer of blubber—nearly half the seal's weight—provides buoyancy, insulation, and reserve energy if the animal must go without food. Fish and shellfish are their favorite meals. Seals can dive deep down into the ocean when fishing.

Seals spend most of the year in the open ocean, returning to land to breed. Seal pups are born in spring and spend several months on land nursing with their mothers. Andre, Rockport's harbormaster and Maine's most famous seal, stars in Lew Dietz's book *Andre*.

sixteen
16

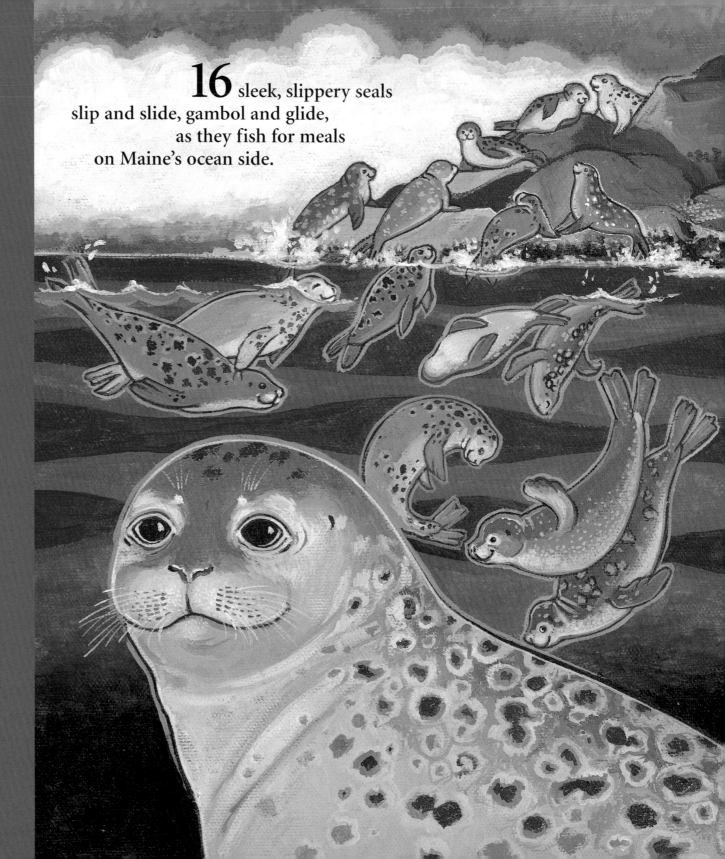

16 sleek, slippery seals
slip and slide, gambol and glide,
as they fish for meals
on Maine's ocean side.

The United Society of Believers was founded in England in 1747. Called "Shaking Quakers" because of their body movements during worship, these people were persecuted. In 1774 led by Mother Ann Lee, they emigrated to America and established their first colony in New Lebanon, New York. Maine's Sabbathday Lake was one of 18 Shaker communities.

Founded in 1783, this community of 200 people dedicated their lives and work to God. On 1,800 acres surrounding Sabbathday Lake, they built a meeting house, communal house, mills, barns, and other farm buildings. They planted orchards and gardens and raised flocks of sheep. Shakers were renowned for their exquisite woodworking skills.

Referred to as "the least of Mother's children in the east," Sabbathday Lake was one of the smallest, poorest, and most isolated Shaker communities, yet today this is the only active group of Shakers remaining in America.

seventeen

17

17 shiny Shaker chairs,
treasured as a family keepsake,
were crafted with painstaking cares
by the Shakers of Sabbathday Lake.

18 picture-perfect pine cones,
Maine's state flowers,
tumble from Eastern white pines,
blown by gusts from autumn showers.

Maine's 17 million acres of forest cover 89 percent of the state's land. These forests are filled with majestic Eastern White Pines, Maine's State Tree, which is the largest cone-bearing tree in the northeastern United States. Its pine cone and tassel are the State Flower.

Eastern White Pine needles are soft, flexible, and grow from two-and-a-half to five inches long. A silvery bluish-green, the needles are grouped in clusters of five. The trees shed these needles at the end of the second growing season. These tall trees have been used to build ships, barns, and houses, and to make paper.

Eastern White Pine cones are slightly curved and measure between four and eight inches. Cone scales are thin and never have prickles. They have a fragrant, gummy resin that sticks to fingers like glue.

eighteen
18

19 cold, captivating clams
burrowing in tidal sands
are dug with a metal rake
just in time for our island clambake.

To a Mainer, there is no finer meal in the world than a clambake. A clambake starts with a big pot of clams steamed over a fire on a beach in the summer, and often includes lobsters, baked potatoes, ears of corn, and melted butter.

Maine fishermen harvest more than 7 million pounds of shellfish every year and clams are among the tastiest. Clams burrow into mud up to two and a half times their shell length by using a muscular "foot." Rounded, grayish-white shells protect the clam. They have a long, extendable siphon, or neck, which allows water containing microscopic plankton to enter the mantle cavity. Here gills trap and transport the food toward the mouth. The fleshy membrane called a mantle also secretes the limy shell. Ridges on shells tell the clam's age. Scientists think thinner lines represent times of stress.

Green crabs, sea stars, birds, fish, whelks, and lobsters enjoy clam dinners as much as we do. Carrying short-handled iron rakes, fishermen comb clamflats in search of these delicacies.

nineteen
19

Maine is home to America's largest black bear population. Shy and anxious to avoid man, more than 21,000 live in our forests and swamps, eating insects, grasses, fish, fruits, nuts, juicy plants, and animals. Their favorite snacks include blueberries, corn, and honey. They are night creatures and use their sense of smell to find food.

Black bears (which may be brown, cinnamon, or black) measure four to seven feet from nose to tail. They have long snouts, small eyes, rounded ears, short tails, and shaggy hair. In winter, mothers give birth to cubs weighing less than a pound. Cubs stay with their mother for two years. Black bears can live more than 30 years. They see colors and have excellent memories and close-up vision. Their hearing is twice as good as a humans. They can swim long distances, run up to 30 miles per hour, and hibernate in caves or hollow trees for months without eating or drinking. University of Maine students are called Black Bears.

twenty
20

20 burly black bears,
big and brawny and brave,
sleep without worries or cares
in a cozy mountain cave.

Because Maine has always depended on the ocean for jobs and food, Maine folk are renowned sailors. To help them travel safely along the rocky and dangerous 3,500 miles of shoreline, 68 lighthouses stand guard. They start with Kittery's Whaleback Light and end with West Quoddy Head Light on the tip of the Eastern Time Zone.

President George Washington commissioned Maine's oldest lighthouse, Portland Head Light. Nearby stands Maine's most powerful beacon, Cape Elizabeth Light. It guides ships into Portland Harbor with the aid of two small lights at Portland Breakwater and Spring Point. Bass Harbor Light directs a unique red beam at the entrance of Blue Hill Bay. Owl's Head Lightstation has witnessed many tragic shipwrecks. So has remote, rockbound Boon Island Light. Storms there were so frequent and brutal that 19th-century fishermen customarily left food and clothes in good weather to help those who would inevitably be wrecked there in foul weather.

thirty
30

30 legendary lighthouses
stand guard on islands and cliffs,
warning of rocks and dangers
to sailors, schooners, and skiffs.

Baked, mashed, scalloped, french-fried, or pan-fried, potatoes are not only nutritious and delicious, but also important to Maine's economy. Maine ranks as one of the nation's top three potato-producing states. These culinary staples are grown predominantly in Maine's Aroostook County, where 64,000 acres are dedicated to the production of potatoes.

The potato is an herb native to Central and South America. While the Spanish were exploring the New World in the 16th century, they brought the potato to Europe. Potatoes are grown best in a moist, cool climate. The plant has oval leaves and violet, pink, or white flowers, which produce a green berry fruit. The potato grows underground. Green potatoes and the leaves of the plant are poisonous if eaten raw.

forty
40

40 practical potatoes,
featured on cooking shows,
are dug from the ground with hoes
long before Aroostook's first snows.

ALL PURPOSE

YUKON GOLD

RED

GOLDRUSH

Baked bean suppers are traditional Saturday night fare in Maine. In early days, Puritan women were forbidden to cook on Sundays, so they slowly baked beans throughout Saturday, ate them for dinner, and offered them to the family for breakfast the next day.

Old-timers all have their favorite recipes, but this one is a winner:

- Soak overnight in cold water: 1 quart navy or pea beans.

- Simmer in same water until tender (2-3 hours). Drain, reserving liquid, and place beans in bean pot in layers: ½ pound chopped salt pork, 1 T salt, 1 large onion, cut into slices.

- Combine 3 T brown sugar, ⅓ cup molasses, 1 tsp. mustard. Pour over beans. Add enough reserved liquid to cover beans. Cover pot. Bake at 300 degrees for 4 hours.

- Remove cover, draw pork to the top, add a little boiling water if beans seem dry, and bake for another 4 hours.

fifty
50

SALE BEAN POTS

50 bountiful baked bean pots,
savory and piping hot,
offer a supper Yankees never boycott.
On Saturdays, baked beans hit the spot.

100 hardworking honeybees
never stop for spelling bees
or summer shopping sprees
while gathering nectar from flowers and trees.

Honeybees originated in tropical Africa then spread north into Europe and west into India and China. They were brought to the Americas by early colonists who used the honey as a sweetener and the bees to pollinate fruit trees. The honeybee is Maine's State Insect.

A typical small hive contains 20,000 bustling bees, divided into queen, drone, and worker bees. The honeybee uses its eyes to spot flowers, its antennae to detect fragrances, its wings for flight, legs for pollen gathering and walking, crop to carry nectar back to the hive, and stinger to defend the hive. Growers bring honeybee hives onto orchards and blueberry barrens to pollinate the blossoms.

one
hundred
100

Cynthia Furlong Reynolds

An eleventh-generation Maine native, Cynthia Furlong Reynolds loves all the back roads, old-timers, and old stories associated with Maine. She is the author of *L is for Lobster: A Maine Alphabet*; *S is for Star: A Christmas Alphabet*; *Our Hometown: America's History Seen Through the Eyes of a Midwestern Village*; and *M is for Maple Syrup: A Vermont Alphabet*, among other books. An award-winning journalist, she has worked on the staffs of several newspapers, Princeton University, and the University of Tampa. As a freelance writer her byline has appeared in dozens of magazines, journals, and newspapers around the country. She lives with her husband, three children, and two dogs in the country outside Ann Arbor, Michigan, but enjoys her summers blueberry-picking, swimming, boating, and fishing on Pleasant River Lake in Maine.

Jeannie Brett

Jeannie Brett has lived in Maine for the past 29 years. She enjoys visiting elementary schools around New England, sharing with both students and educators her original artwork, her love of the natural world, and her excitement about the process of illustrating children's books. Jeannie studied at the School of the Museum of Fine Arts in Boston and at the Minneapolis College of Art and Design. She lives in York, Maine, with her husband Greg, and their three children, Gregory, Sophie, and Lee. They share their home with a horse named Bailey, a wonderful Newfoundland, Cali, and two enormous cats (brothers) Macaroni and Tortellini. As well as a lengthy list of independent, illustrative work, *Fishing for Numbers* is her third children's book published by Sleeping Bear Press along with *M is for Mayflower :A Massachusetts Alphabet* and *L is for Lobster: A Maine Alphabet*. She is also a contributor to *P is for Passport: A World Alphabet*.